For my dearest kin, Robert and Peter—D. L.

For Rez, Fritzy, and Nova, and the many, many creatures
that have found their way to Lindsay Wildlife Hospital,
and the hardworking staff and volunteers who help
them—S. L.

BEACH LANE BOOKS • An imprint of Simon & Schuster Children's Publishing Division • 1230 Avenue of the Americas, New York, New York 10020 • Text copyright © 2018 by Diane Lang • Illustrations copyright © 2018 by Stephanie Laberis • All rights reserved, including the right of reproduction in whole or in part in any form. • BEACH LANE BOOKS is a trademark of Simon & Schuster, Inc. • For information about special discounts for bulk purchases, please contact Simon & Schuster Special Sales at 1-866-506-1949 or business@simonandschuster.com. • The Simon & Schuster Speakers Bureau can bring authors to your live event. For more information or to book an event, contact the Simon & Schuster Speakers Bureau at 1-866-248-3049 or visit our website at www.simonspeakers.com. • Book design by Lauren Rille • The text for this book was set in Neutra. • Manufactured in China • 0218 SCP • First Edition • 10 9 8 7 6 5 4 3 2 1 • CIP data for this book is available from the Library of Congress. • ISBN 978-1-4814-4709-6 (hardcover) • ISBN 978-1-4814-4710-2 (eBook)

written by
DIANE LANG

illustrated by
STEPHANIE LABERIS

Fur, Feather, Fin
ALL OF US ARE KIN

BEACH LANE BOOKS • New York   London   Toronto   Sydney   New Delhi

All animals on Earth are kin,
while not the same outside or in.
Some we stroke with loving hand;
some we don't yet understand.

But we're all linked in families
with variations such as these . . .

MAMMALS

Milk to drink and furry hide,
mammals keep warm from inside.

Their babies are not hatched; they're born,
no matter where their fur is worn.

All need a parent when they're new . . .

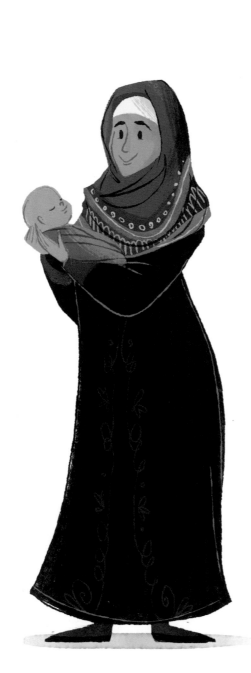

like humans—yes, we're mammals, too!

BIRDS

Feathers keep birds warm and dry,
giving them the shape to fly.

Some will soar; some probe the sand.
Flightless ones live life on land.
Some seek nectar in each bloom.

Those who hunt will watch . . .

AMPHIBIANS

Changing body; smooth, moist skin—
that is an amphibian.
Metamorphosis: the road
for changing tadpole into toad . . .

or salamander,

frog,

or newt.

And at the end, a whole new suit!

REPTILES

Reptiles' dry and scaly skin
keeps the warmth from outside in.

Snakes and lizards seek the sun
as basking turtles long have done.

Some have a smooth and graceful glide . . .

some run
or climb
or dig
to hide!

ARTHROPODS

Arthropods have hard outsides,
jointed legs, and varied lives.
Some will live beneath the seas,

while others lightly ride the breeze.

From insects, chewing on a stem...

to spiders, who are eating them!

FISH

Fish have bones—plus gills to get
oxygen from where it's wet.
Some have shapes somewhat alike,

like salmon,

trout,

catfish,

or pike,

but some are shaped a different way . . .

such as seahorse,

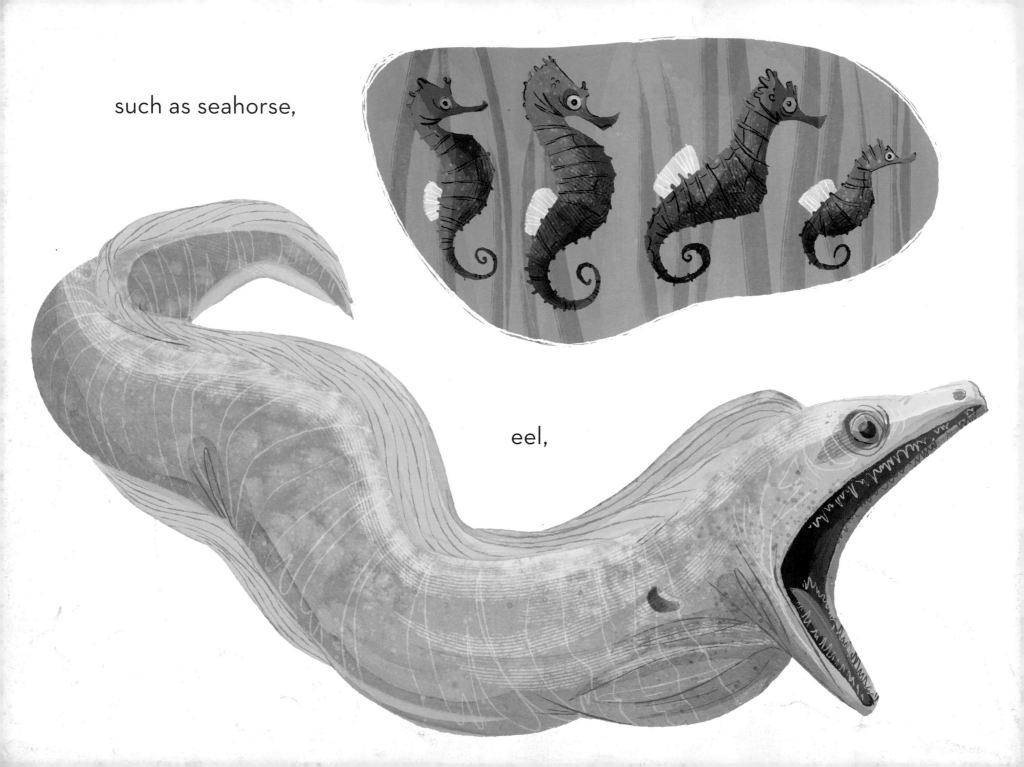

eel,

or ray.

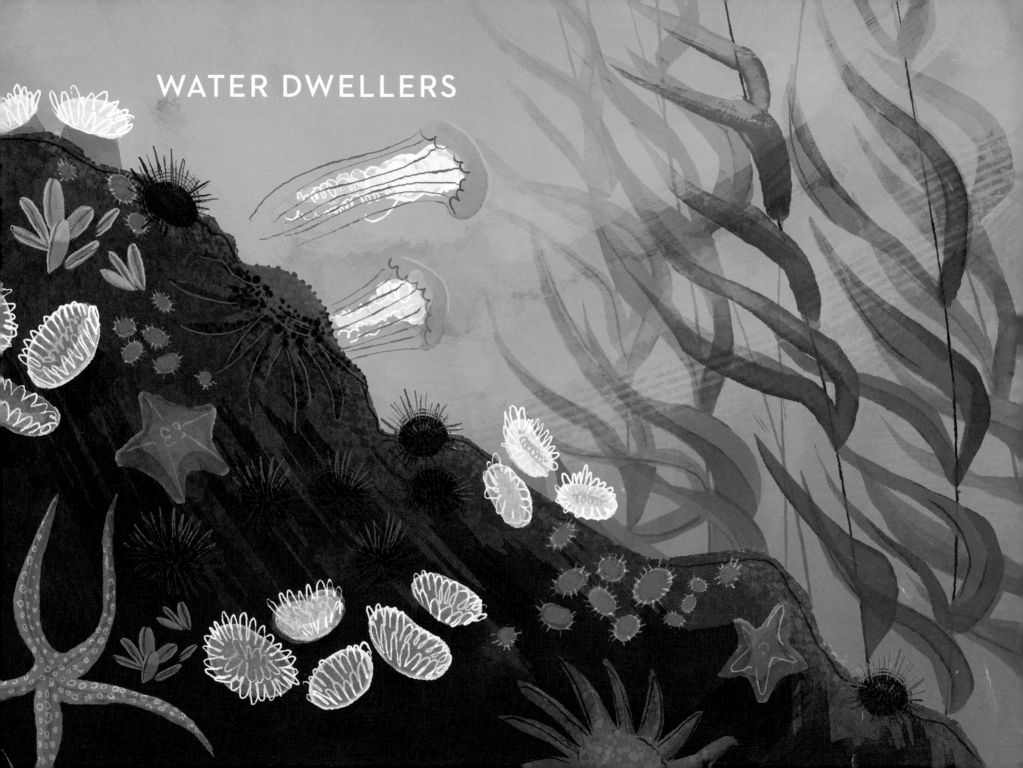

WATER DWELLERS

More water dwellers live offshore,
in tidal pools, on ocean floor.
Some cling to rocks, while some float free,
our sandy, salty family.

With tentacles
or fins
or spines . . .

life under water intertwines.

DETRITIVORES

Detritivores, so oft forgotten,
dine on things both dead and rotten.

Worms and bugs make their dessert
of rot into the richest dirt.
Underground or deep in bark . . .

they're heroes of the damp and dark.

From lofty height to humble base,
every creature has a place,
as well as needs like food, fresh air,
a place of safety—nest or lair.

And while we're different here on Earth,
in eating, moving, giving birth,
common things make us complete:

minds that work and hearts that beat.

ALL OF US ARE KIN.

What does that mean? How are we the same?

All of us—people and other animals—are like a big, diverse family. How? Not only do we share the land, water, and other resources of this planet, but our bodies have developed to work in many similar (sometimes identical) ways, from legs and eyes to hearts and brains. Maybe most important, people have desires and needs in common with many, many other animals: safety, concern for our young, a proper home, access to food and water, and much more.

To meet these needs, we need one another—yes, animals need other animals (and not just as part of the food web). Hummingbirds need spider silk to make their nests strong and stretchy. Other birds need woodpeckers to make holes in trees for their nests. Salamanders need ground squirrels to make shady burrows in which to hide.

Who do we need? We need earthworms and all the tiny bugs that make healthy soil so we can grow plants for food. We need bees to pollinate the plants. We need bats to gobble up grain-eating moths (and mosquitoes!). And other animals need us—to pick up plastic bags and other trash that might look like food to them, to understand that poisons go up the food chain (and therefore, avoid using them), and to keep learning about the value of all life. There are countless ways that we depend on one another. We have many different looks—that's for sure—but we have much in common, and as people, we can observe, understand, and improve the lives of all the other animals. Lucky us!

How are we different?

While we have much in common, we are also very different! Most of the animal groups in this book are called "classes." Here are some of the differences between them, in the order that they appear in the book:

Mammals are the animals who have fur or hair, give live birth (don't lay eggs—except the platypus and echidna), and nurse their babies. *There*

are around 4,000 different kinds of mammals in the world. We are one of them.

Birds are truly our feathered friends. All birds have feathers (even if they don't fly), and only birds have feathers. Feathers keep birds warm, dry, protected, camouflaged, and much more. *There are about 10,000 different kinds of birds in the world!*

Amphibians are the frogs, toads, and salamanders. They have smooth skin (no fur, feathers, or scales), and they lay squishy eggs in fresh water or wet places. Once the babies hatch, they experience big changes—such as growing legs—in going from tadpole, or larva, to adult, in a process called metamorphosis. *There are 7,000 different kinds of amphibians in the world, and most of them are frogs.*

Reptiles are the scaly, dry guys (unless they happen to be in the water, such as sea turtles and pond turtles). Reptiles have some form of scales on their bodies, and they all breathe air (even the swimmers) and lay their eggs on dry land. They include snakes, lizards, turtles, and alligators. *There are almost 10,000 kinds of reptiles in the world!*

Arthropods are the creepy crawlies: insects, spiders, centipedes, beetles, or any creature (some very small) who has a hard outside (exoskeleton) instead of bones inside, and has legs with joints. Some live on land; some, such as lobsters and crabs, live in the water. *Most kinds of animals in the world are arthropods! There are at least a million different kinds (maybe even ten million!), and most of them are insects.*

Fish are our watery neighbors—the ones who must get oxygen from the water through their gills. They all have bones, and most of them have the usual "fish" shape, but there are others who are shaped differently, such as seahorses and eels. *There are 30,000 different kinds of fish in the world!*

The water-dwelling animals mentioned in this book—the ones who are not in the classes listed above—belong to many different classes, and describing all of these groups would take a whole new book! From urchins to octopuses to snails to jellies to clams, some live in the ocean, some in lakes, rivers, streams, or marshes. They may have spines, tentacles (long, flexible arms), shells, or many other eye-catching looks.

Detritivores are not a class of animal, but rather a group of various animals that do the same important job: eating and breaking down dead plants and animals into small bits so that the nutrients inside can become part of a healthy soil. Detritivores include worms, snails, flies, cockroaches, millipedes, earwigs, pill bugs, springtails, and many other tiny creatures.

Note to teachers: You may have noticed that the first two lines of each animal class (mammals, birds, amphibians, reptiles, arthropods, and fish—plus detritivores) can be stand-alone definitions; they were written as easy memory guides.

We can help animals right now! How?

- Throw away or recycle all litter, plastic bags, and other trash, and keep the trash can lid on tight.
- Don't feed wild animals. The food they find themselves is *much* healthier for them. And spread the word that bread is very harmful to ducks.
- If you go fishing, pick up every little bit of fishing line—plus any hooks, of course.
- Keep your cat indoors. Outdoor cats kill billions of songbirds and other

small animals every year. Yes, even the sweetest cats; it's just what nature tells them to do. Besides, your cat will be healthier indoors.
- Put decals on your windows (or hang something nearby) to keep birds from crashing into them. Birds often can't tell what is real nature and what is a reflection.
- Avoid poisons and sticky traps. They end up hurting many, many other animals besides pests.
- Protect waterways by never putting anything down storm drains, which connect directly to streams, bays, or oceans.

Want to learn more?

You are in luck! There are many wonderful books and websites where you can find out more about animals.

Books: Visit your library or bookstore and ask for the section on animals. You will find hundreds of books on the topic! Two favorites are:
Wildlife of the World (DK Publishing, 2015)
Animal! (DK Publishing, 2016)

Websites:
Animal Diversity: animaldiversity.org
Cornell Laboratory of Ornithology: allaboutbirds.org
DK Animals: dkfindout.com/us/animals-and-nature
San Diego Zoo: animals.sandiegozoo.org/animals
My website has many activities for you to download: dianelang.net